HKJC

25 Fun Things to Do on a RAINY DAY

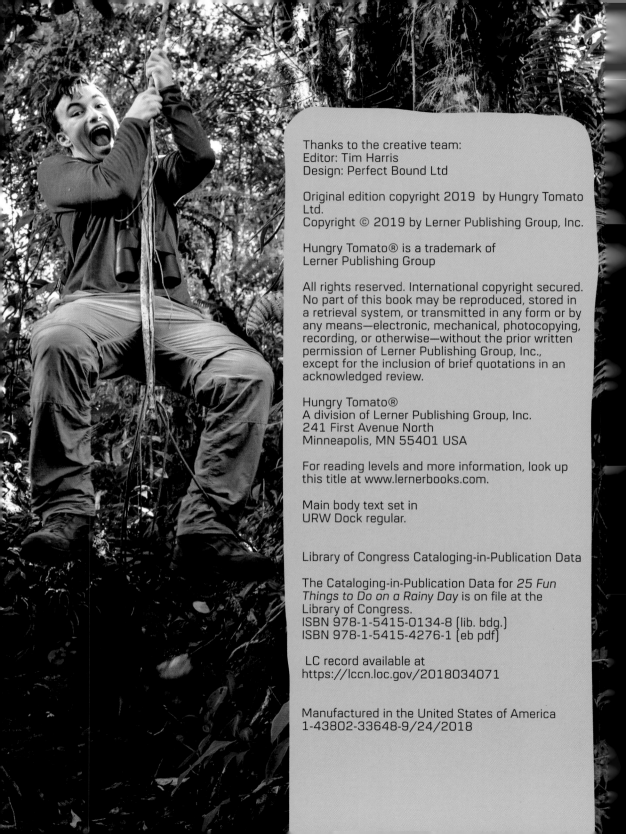

Thanks to the creative team:
Editor: Tim Harris
Design: Perfect Bound Ltd

Original edition copyright 2019 by Hungry Tomato Ltd.
Copyright © 2019 by Lerner Publishing Group, Inc.

Hungry Tomato® is a trademark of Lerner Publishing Group

Hungry Tomato®
A division of Lerner Publishing Group, Inc.
241 First Avenue North
Minneapolis, MN 55401 USA

For reading levels and more information, look up this title at www.lernerbooks.com.

Main body text set in
URW Dock regular.

Library of Congress Cataloging-in-Publication Data

The Cataloging-in-Publication Data for *25 Fun Things to Do on a Rainy Day* is on file at the Library of Congress.
ISBN 978-1-5415-0134-8 [lib. bdg.]
ISBN 978-1-5415-4276-1 [eb pdf]

LC record available at
https://lccn.loc.gov/2018034071

Manufactured in the United States of America
1-43802-33648-9/24/2018

25 Fun Things to Do on a

RAINY DAY

PAUL MASON

HUNGRY TOMATO™

MINNEAPOLIS

CONTENTS

Don't be down on a rainy day!

You might think waking up to a rainy day is a bit sad—but don't be down. There are LOTS of things to do on a rainy day.

RAINY-DAY GEAR

An umbrella will keep you mostly dry on a rainy day, if there is no wind. For full protection, though, you need:

- Waterproof hat, coat, and pants
- Rain boots

INDOORS

If you stay indoors, it's a good idea to look busy. Otherwise you might be told to do something like:

- clean your room
- do the dishes
- vacuum the carpets
- clean the bathroom

Fortunately, there are plenty of better indoor ideas in this book. Some are quiet and can be done on your own. A few are noisy and need a group of friends. Some are quick, and others take hours—or even days. Whatever you feel like doing, there should be an idea here for you.

OUTDOORS

Of course, going out in the rain is unlikely to hurt you. If you have the right clothes it can even be pretty fun. So we have also included some rainy-days ideas for outside, too.

RAINY DAY ONLY

Some things can only happen on a rainy day, so a few of the activities here are things that you can only do when the rain is pouring down.

1. Make Money from Old Things

A rainy day is a good opportunity to earn some cash by selling your old things.

1 **Clear out your space.** Decide what you are going to sort through: old clothes, toys, books, sports equipment, or anything else you can think of.

Get everything out and decide what to sell. If you haven't used something for a year, do you still need it?

2 **Work out your prices.** Make a list of your prices. If something is rare or very popular (such as a first edition of the first-ever *Harry Potter* book) it might be worth a lot. If it is in poor condition it will be worth less.

Type of item:	Good-condition value
Sports equipment	30% of new cost
Books	10–15% of new cost
Clothes	10% of new cost
Toys	10% of new cost

You could sell your items in a garage sale. Or you could ask a teacher to organize a market at school.

STAY SAFE

If you are planning to sell your things online, ask an adult to post the ad for you.

If you want to sell your stuff at a garage sale, make sure an adult knows what you are doing and comes along if they think it is necessary.

2. Write Your Pet's Life Story

If you don't have pets, don't worry. It's even more fun writing about an imaginary pet. How about a pet crocodile, honey badger, or pterodactyl?

1 **Research your pet.** Find out a bit about your pet. If it's a dachshund, what were dachshunds originally bred for? Or a gerbil: where did gerbils come from?

This information will help you write your pet's character.

2 **Make a timeline.** Now make a timeline of the pet's life: when it was born, when it came to live with you, and the date now.

Add other events that your pet was around for (such as a birthday party, wedding, or someone being ill). What would these have been like from the pet's point of view?

3 **Use your imagination.** Now you can write your pet's life story, combining big events in its life with things it might have witnessed.

> Use your imagination! The great thing about pets is they never say you got the story wrong.

3. Make Your Own Comic

ALL YOU NEED:

- Imagination
- Paper (lots)
- Pencils and pens
- Eraser

Making your own comic can easily take a whole day (or more). But if it looks like the sun might come out soon, you can also make it a quick activity.

1 **Find a subject.** What is your comic going to be about? Here are some other subjects (but feel free to choose your own):
- Discovering you have superpowers
- A bully getting what they deserve
- Your pet
- A boring lesson that goes wrong in a funny way

2 **Develop a storyline.** Now turn your basic idea into a storyline, divided up into periods of time. Say you're making a cartoon of your pet's life story:
- **A** Max is one of six dachshund puppies.
- **B** Max comes to live at his new home with us.
- **C** He grows up.
- **D** Max is now four years old.

3 **Think of drawings.** What will you draw for each stage of your story?

You might have lots of things you want to draw about Max coming to live with you (he peed on the floor, he slept on your bed, he went for his first walk on the leash).

Make quick sketches of each scene and lay them out. Do they tell the story as you imagined?

4 **Plan your storyboard**. The next step is to decide how to lay out your cartoon. Some of the pictures might be funny or full of action and need lots of space—maybe even a full page.

Draw out the panels on each page, showing where each drawing goes and how big it will be.

5 **Add drawings**. Once you are happy with the layout, add the drawings (based on the sketches you did earlier) and words. Sometimes, it's a good idea to add the words first.

6 **Color in.** Adding color will make your comic really stand out.

7 **Draw a cover.** The last step is to name your comic and draw a cover for it. Once this is finished, staple or fold the whole comic together and it is finished.

ONLINE COMIC CREATION

There are comic-book websites that can be fun to use: try pixton.com or toondoo.com, for example. We think it's more fun to do the whole process yourself on paper, though!

1

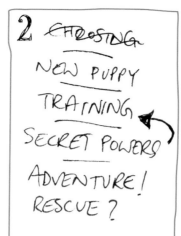

2 CHOOSING
NEW PUPPY
TRAINING
SECRET POWERS
ADVENTURE!
RESCUE?

3

4 SUPER NOODLE
POW
THE END

5

6

Don't forget to leave space to add words!

SUPER NOODLE!

4. Play Threes

Threes is a card game. Once you learn the rules it is very difficult to stop playing. The basic idea is to get rid of all your cards as soon as you can.

1 Deal. Deal out three cards per player, face down. Then deal three on top of these, face up. Finally, deal each player three more cards face down, which they can pick up.

If they want to, players can now swap picked-up cards with face-up ones.

2 Play. The player with a black 3 goes first. If no one has one, it's the player with a red 3, a black 4, red 4, etc.

The first player lays down a card, then picks one up from the cards that didn't get dealt. The player to their left then has to lay a card with the same value or higher.

Except . . .

3 Picking up. If a player cannot go, they have to pick up the whole pile of cards and add them to their hand.

4 Out. Once all the cards in the leftover pile are gone, you play the cards in your hand, then the ones lying face up, then the ones lying face down. You cannot look at what the face-down cards are before playing them. If the card is lower than the last card played, you must pick up the pile.

When all your cards are gone, you are out. The last player still in loses.

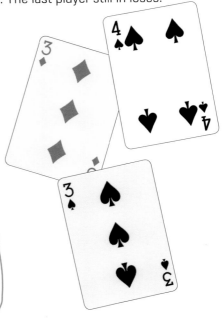

SPECIAL CARDS

- 2s can always be put down
- 4s can always be put down and have the same value as the card beneath them
- on a 7, the next player has to lay the same (or lower)
- 10s can always be played: the whole pile is taken out and the player lays a new card

5. Go for an Outdoor Swim (You're wet anyway . . .)

ALL YOU NEED

- Swimsuit
- Towel
- Warm clothes

On a really rainy day, you can't go for a hike, a bike ride, or a visit to the park. What you could do, though, is go swimming outside.

1 **Pick a spot.** One of the best places for an outdoor swim is an open-air pool. You can get changed inside—your clothes will still be dry when you get out.

2 **Check the temperature.** Splash a bit of water onto your chest and face to make sure the water is not too cold.

3 **Feet first entry.** In a pool, follow the lifeguard's instructions for getting in. Anywhere else, always get in feet first. Every year people hurt themselves by diving into unfamiliar water.

4 **Enjoy your swim!** Floating on your back with the rain falling on your face and rainwater trickling into your mouth is a great feeling.

WATER SAFETY

Never swim in the sea, a lake, or a river unless you are 100% sure it's safe. Make sure one of your parents knows where you are going and has said it's OK.

6. Do an Experiment

ALL YOU NEED

- Large bowl
- Cornstarch (16 oz.)
- Water (2 cups)
- Spoon
- Clear, resealable plastic bag
- An egg (uncooked)
- Food dye

When is a liquid not a liquid? When it's something called a non-Newtonian liquid, that's when. This experiment will show you how these liquids work.

1 **Mix ingredients.** Put the cornstarch into the bowl. Add the water and mix it in using your fingers. (Adding food dye to the water first makes colored slime.)

2 **Get the mixture right.** Keep mixing until the slimy liquid is like runny honey. If it's not quite thick enough, add more cornstarch to make the slime thicker. If it's too thick, adding more water will make it thinner.

Now you are ready to do some experiments.

3 **Scoop it.** Scoop some of the slime into your hand and roll it into a ball. As long as you keep pressure on it, it stays ball-shaped. Stop pressing, though, and it will flow back into the bowl.

4 **Hit it.** Try quickly punching the surface of the slime. Most fluids would splash, but not this one. Your punch's force pushes water away, leaving just a dense patch of cornstarch below your fist.

5 **Do one last eggs-periment.** Spoon some of the slime into the resealable bag until it is two-thirds full. Now gently push an uncooked egg into the mixture.

Make sure the bag is really tightly sealed, then find somewhere you can safely drop it from about three yards up.

Now drop the bag—what happens to the egg?

MESS ALERT
Making cornstarch slime can get messy. Of course, that might not bother you.

NON-NEWTONIAN LIQUID DISPOSAL

If you pour your slime down the sink when you're done, there is a good chance it will block the pipes, and you'll be in big trouble. To avoid this, spoon the mixture into a sealable bag (or two) and put it in the garbage.

In a normal, Newtonian liquid such as water, the egg would break. In this non-Newtonian liquid, though, as the bag hits the ground the slime becomes solid around the egg. The force of the landing is evenly distributed around the shell's surface and it stays intact.

7. Make a Kite

ALL YOU NEED

- Thick plastic bags (at least 40 x 20 in.)
- Scissors
- Flying line from a kite shop
- Electrical tape
- 2 x wooden 3/16-in. dowel, 40 in. in length
- Marker

Sure, you could go to a shop and buy a kite. But making a simple one is quite easy, and flying a kite you made yourself is super fun.

1 Mark out your kite. Measure 40 inches along the side of one bag and put a dot at each end. Measure down 10 inches, then 20 inches in, and mark that place with a dot, too. Draw lines between the top, middle, and bottom dots.

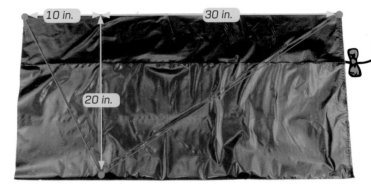

10 in.   30 in.

20 in.

2 Cut out the shape. Cut out along the two lines, then open up the shape: this is your kite.

3 Add the spars. Lay a piece of dowel from the tip to the tail of the shape. Fold a 4-inch length of tape over the dowel and onto the plastic to hold each end in place. Repeat for the cross spar.

5 **Add a tail.** Tape together bits of plastic to make a tail at least 16 feet long and tie it to the bottom of the kite.

4 **Tie on the line.** Poke a small hole in the plastic where the two spars cross. Push the flying line through and tie it securely around the spars (crisscross around them four times to be sure they are tied together).

That's it: your kite is ready to fly!

8. Say Hello in Five Languages

Knowing a few words in a foreign language can come in handy. The first word most people learn in a new language is "hello."

Here's how to say hello in five of the world's six most commonly spoken languages. (We left out English, the third most common language. If you are reading this, you must already know that one.)

1 **Mandarin Chinese.**
Saying hello: *Nǐ hǎo*
Sounds like: **NEE how**

2 **Spanish.**
Saying hello: *Hola*
Sounds like: **OH-laa**

4 **Hindi.**
Saying hello: *Namaste*
Sounds like: **NAM-ahs-tay**

5 **Arabic.**
Saying hello: *marHaban*
Sounds like: **mer-HAB-ben**

6 **Portuguese.**
Saying hello: *Olá!*
Sounds like: **OH-la**

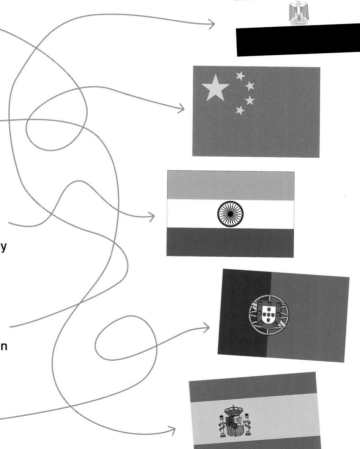

9. Learn Some Makaton

Makaton is a simple, international form of communication. It is sometimes used by people with autism or Down syndrome, but anyone can learn it.

**GOOD
OK
HELLO**
Using both hands means "very good."

GOOD MORNING
A thumbs-up followed by touching your chest with your fingertips

GOODBYE
Wave your hand from side to side

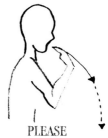

**PLEASE
THANK YOU**
Please is halfway down; thank you is down to stomach level

YES
Tilted forward from the wrist

NO
Hand waved out to the side

COME
Index finger moves in the direction requested

GO
Index finger moves in the direction requested

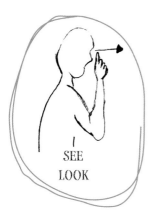

**SEE
LOOK**

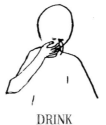

DRINK

SLEEP

DINNER
Bring your right hand to your mouth twice, with the fingertips touching

10. Write a Team Poem

This is a fun activity to do with up to four friends. You are going to write a five-line poem called a limerick together.

Remember, limericks are sometimes called nonsense poems—so your poem doesn't have to make total sense. The first, second, and fifth lines have eight or nine syllables, and the third and fourth lines have five or six.

1 **Pick a subject.** One of you picks a subject and says or writes the first line to start things off:

I'd rather have fingers than toes.

2 **Rhyme the last word.** The next person makes up the second line, ending with a word that rhymes.

I'd rather have eyes than a nose.

3 **Introduce a new rhyme.** The third line must not rhyme with the two that went before:

And as for my teeth

4 **Add a line.** The fourth player's line rhymes with the one before (teeth):

It's my strong belief

5 **Back to the start.** The last line should rhyme with the first two (toes and nose):

I'll be terribly sad when they goes.

This is not good English—but it is a good limerick.

11. Go on a Damp-Day Creature Hunt

Sometimes you've just GOT to get outside. Why not take someone on a hunt to discover which creatures don't mind when it's wet?

ALL YOU NEED
- Waterproof clothes
- Notepad and pencil
- Camera

1 **Pick an area.** Decide where to explore. Somewhere close by might be best, just in case you get completely soaked.

Will you do your creature hunt in the woods, a grassy area, or on a city street? There are animals in all of them.

2 **Take photos and notes.** First, just wait and look around. What animals can you see? There will probably be birds, flying insects, pets, and maybe more. Take photos and notes. For example:

Photo 1: brown freckled bird, pointy beak
Behavior: pecking at grass
Notes: puffed-up feathers

After a while you could start exploring more. Look under rocks, in bushes, and even on buildings.

3 **Research what you have found.** When you get home, use your notes and photos to find out more about the animals you saw. Why were the bird's feathers puffed up, for example?

STAY SAFE
If you are exploring outside, make sure an adult knows where you are going and what time you will be back.

12. Visit a Museum

A rainy day is a really good excuse to visit places you might not normally go—such as a little local museum you have always wondered about.

1 **Choose a museum.** First, you need to pick a museum to visit. Local councils can often tell you about nearby museums—and if you are lucky, it will be a quirky one.

> In Ulm, Germany, there's a museum of bread.

> In Maidstone, England, they have a Dog Collar Museum.

> Maybe strangest is the Museum of Barbed Wire in La Crosse, Kansas.

2 **Check the details.** Find out when the museum is open and whether you have to pay to go in. You also need to work out how to get there.

3 **Food and drink.** Depending on how far away the museum is, you could plan a packed lunch or find out if it has a café.

13. Create a Home Cinema

ALL YOU NEED

- TV and DVD/Blu-ray player
- Snacks
- Drinks
- Lots of cushions, pillows, and blankets
- Camping/yoga mats (optional)

Going to the movies with your friends is expensive. Maybe instead you could stay home and create a cinema with a twist!

1 **Pick a movie.** Actually, pick two, then ask your guests which one they would prefer. (With a choice of more than two they might never agree . . .)

2 **Arrange snacks and drinks.** Ask an adult what you can offer everyone to eat and drink. Maybe you could have:
- Sandwiches
- Popcorn
- Juice
- Pieces of fruit

3 **Set up the room.** This is a cinema with a difference: you will all be lying down. Everyone needs at least two cushions or pillows and a blanket. Camping or yoga mats will make the floor softer.

4 **Start the movie.** Once everyone is settled in their spots, click play, lie back, and enjoy the movie.

14. Become a Yogi

A yogi is a person who does yoga. Yoga is a kind of exercise using strength, flexibility, and breathing. It can easily be done indoors.

1 **Lie down.** Lying down is a yoga position called corpse pose. Lie on your back with your arms at your sides. Let your back relax against the floor. Stretch each leg away from you, then relax it.

2 **Breathe in, then out.** Breathe in deeply, letting your ribs and belly rise up as your lungs fill with air. Then breathe out slowly. Wait a moment before breathing in again. Do at least 10 deep breaths like this.

3 **Cat pose.** Kneel down with your toes pointing out behind you, then put your hands on the floor in front. They should be straight underneath your shoulders and your knees straight under your hips. Look at the floor.

   Breathe in deeply. As you breathe out, bend your backbone toward the ceiling. When you breathe in again, slowly return to your starting position.

4 **Cow pose.** This has the same starting position as cat pose. As you breathe in, try to lift your chest and bottom toward the ceiling. This will drop your belly toward the floor. When you breathe out, slowly return to your starting position.

5 **Downward dog pose.** Start as in the cow and cat poses, but with your hands a bit further forward. Breathe out and lift your knees off the floor. Lift your bottom toward the ceiling. You are aiming to make a straight line from your hands to your bottom, and another from your bottom to your heels.

WATCH OUT

Never do a yoga pose so that it hurts or feels like it is stretching you too much. If you ever feel uncomfortable, stop and gently return to a better position.

15. Make Some Treats

Maybe before your home cinema event (page 21), you could make some treats for your guests. Everyone loves rice-pop cakes:

1 **Melt.** Put the chocolate, butter, and corn syrup into a heat-proof bowl and melt it. You can do this in 10-second bursts in a microwave, or by putting the bowl over a pot of boiling water.

2 **Stir.** Stir in the puffed rice. Some people add a few raisins or slices of dried apricot at this point, too.

3 **Make cakes.** Now divide your mixture into nine roughly equal parts and put them in cupcake holders. Put the cakes in the fridge for an hour until they are cool and ready to eat.

INGREDIENTS:

- 2/3 cup milk chocolate chips
- 1/3 cup dark chocolate chips
- 1/2 cup butter
- 4 tablespoons of corn syrup
- 4 cups puffed rice
- Paper cupcake holders

HELP NEEDED

This recipe involves hot liquids. Always ask an adult to help, or at least watch what you are doing, when making this recipe.

16. Write a Play

ALL YOU NEED

- Pen and paper, or a computer, to write things down

If a group of you is trapped by the rain, how about spending an afternoon writing a play?

1 Pick a subject. What is your play about? It could be a real event or a made-up one, but make it an interesting challenge (a mysterious theft, perhaps).

2 Decide the characters and setting. Make a list of the characters and what they are like. They could be historical figures, scientists, robbers, or something else. Knowing what they are like will help you write their lines later.

Where is the play set? Is it where the theft took place, at the police station, or even in the getaway car?

3 Make a plot. Try this plan for your plot, separating the play into four parts:
- **A:** introduction to the characters and the challenge they face
- **B:** events get more exciting . . . leading to a crucial dramatic moment
- **C:** what happens after the crucial moment, as things begin to slow down again
- **D:** how things end

4 Write the lines. Finally, use your plot to write what each character says and when they say it.

17. Produce a Play

TOP TIP: In warm, dry weather, somewhere outside with blankets and cushions can be a great place to put on a play.

ALL YOU NEED

- A play
- Costumes
- Props
- Space
- An audience

Having written a play (page 24), you probably want to perform it. Getting ready to do this is called producing it.

1 **Hold auditions.** Auditions are where each person speaks the same lines by a character. Other people watch, then decide who is best for that role.

DIRECTOR

2 **Costumes and props.** Next you need to arrange costumes and props. Choosing your costume can be a great excuse to rummage around in the dress-up box.

Props are the items actors need to play a part. Make a list of all the props you need. They could be things like a detective's badge, a wand, or a bottle of (not-really) poisoned water.

3 **Set up the stage.** Decide where the play is going to be performed. Questions to ask:
- Is there enough space?
- Where will the actors come on stage from?
- Is there room for the audience to sit comfortably?

4 **Check lighting.** After all your work, it is important that the audience can see the actors. Make sure they are well lit.

5 **Rehearse.** Rehearsing your play will help the actors remember their lines. It also helps to show if there is anything you have forgotten.

6 **Perform!** It might take quite a few rainy days before you are ready, but finally it will be time to gather your audience and perform the play.

18. Play Rain Racers

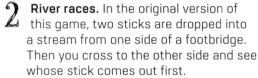

The force of gravity means water flows downhill. It does not always flow at the same speed, though. This makes it possible to hold rain races with your friends.

Here are some possible rain races:

1 **Window races.** This is the simplest rain race and is a very quick activity. You and your friends each pick a raindrop that is near the top of the window. As soon as you pick, the race starts. Whose raindrop gets to the bottom first?

2 **River races.** In the original version of this game, two sticks are dropped into a stream from one side of a footbridge. Then you cross to the other side and see whose stick comes out first.

If you do not have a footbridge nearby, or want the race to be a bit longer, just throw your sticks in the stream at a starting point, then run to a finish line further downstream and see who wins.

> You don't need to go to the countryside to race your sticks.

SAFETY CHECK

If you are playing near moving water (a stream or river), make sure an adult knows where you are going to be and has given you permission.

19. Go Cloud Spotting

If there is one thing you can be guaranteed on a rainy day, it is that there will be lots of clouds around. It's a good time to do some cloud spotting:

High clouds

Cirrus. High up, wispy clouds that look thin and stretched out.

CLOUDS

HIGH	Cirrocumulus / Cirrus
23 000 ft / 7 000 m	
MID	Cumulonimbus / Altostratus / Stratus / Altocumulus / Nimbostratus
6 500 ft / 2 000 m	
LOW	Cumulus / Stratocumulus

Middle clouds

Altostratus. Thin clouds through which the sun can almost be seen.

Altocumulus. These clouds are thin like altostratus, but more broken up in shape.

Low clouds

Cumulus. Cumulus clouds are heaped up or puffy looking (a bit like cauliflower).

Nimbostratus. Flat-bottomed and heavy, these clouds deliver steady rain.

Cumulonimbus. Flat-bottomed clouds (often in the shape of an anvil) that stretch high up into the atmosphere. They can deliver lightning and heavy rain showers.

20. Measure Rainfall

On weather reports you might have heard people say things like, "There was 3 inches of rain last night." How do they know? They use a rain gauge—and now you can, too.

1 **Prepare the bottle.** To let water in, the top eight inches of the bottle need to be cut off in as straight a line as possible.

2 **Cut the funnel to size.** Adding a funnel stops water evaporating and means you will get a more accurate result.

First, put the funnel into the top of the bottle. If it doesn't fit, use the marker pen to draw a line on the funnel where the top edge of the bottle touches it. Remove the funnel and cut along this line, then put the funnel back. It should now fit in the top of the bottle with no overlap.

3 **Add pebbles and water.** Now add about four inches of pebbles to the bottom of the bottle. These are to stop your rain gauge blowing over in wind. Next, pour just enough water into the bottle to completely cover the pebbles.

4 **Mark off the gauge.** Use a ruler to mark off half inch intervals, starting with zero inches at the level of the water and going almost to the top of the bottle.

5 **Put your rain gauge outside.** Find a spot where there is nothing except sky above the gauge. If you can find a place that's also out of the wind and direct sunlight, that is even better.

6 **Record your data.** If you want to know how much rain has fallen each hour, check the level every hour. (You could record daily or weekly rainfall instead, but it should always be an equal amount of time between checks.) Write down when the result was recorded and how much rain fell, like this:

Monday June 3, 6:00 P.M.: 0.75 in.
Tuesday June 4, 6:00 P.M.: 1.5 in.

Once you have recorded each result, tip the water (but not the pebbles) out of the gauge and top it back up to the zero mark.

7 **Make a rainfall graph.** Once you have all the results you want, make a graph. Along the bottom, put the times (the hour, day, or week). Up the side, put the amount of rain that fell into your gauge. Mark your results on the graph. You can present them as a line, bar graph, or bar chart.

WATCH OUT

The cutting parts of this activity need a lot of force, so ask an adult to help you.

1

2

3

Also make sure you have permission to cut up the funnel.

4

5

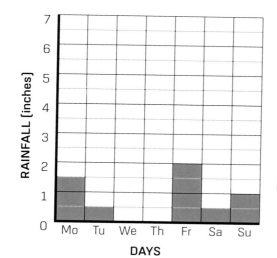

21-25. Five More Things . . .

Here are five more things to try on a rainy day. For one or two of them you will need help (usually help getting there or paying).

21 **Set up indoor circuit training**
You need someone with a big home for this! You could burn off some energy with sit-ups in the kitchen, push-ups in the living room, star jumps in a bedroom, and running up and down stairs between each set of exercises.

22 **Learn mirror writing**
Mirror writing means the words only make sense when you look at them in reverse. Use a small mirror to practice writing your name in reverse. Then start learning other letters.

23 **Send coded messages**
First you need to make up a code, of course. A simple one is to write out the alphabet, then write numbers 1–26 above the letters. Now you have a simple number code.

1	2	3	4	5	6	7	8	9
A	B	C	D	E	F	G	H	I
10	11	12	13	14	15	16	17	18
J	K	L	M	N	O	P	Q	R
19	20	21	22	23	24	25	26	
S	T	U	V	W	X	Y	Z	

8-5-12-12-15

24 **Decorate yourself**
Not your actual self—an outline of it. Lie on a roll of art paper or some leftover cardboard, then get someone to draw around you. Use glue to stick down old bits of cloth or sweet wrappers to fill in the outline.

25 **Go ice skating**
If there is an indoor ice rink near you, it will probably be quieter than normal on a rainy day. After all, most people stay in when it's raining!

I wish it were sunny outside!

Index

Picture Credits

THE AUTHOR

*Paul Mason is a prolific author of children's
books, many award-nominated, on such subjects
as how to save the planet, gross things that go
wrong with the human body, and the world's
craziest inventors. Many include surprising,
unbelievable, or just plain disgusting facts. Today,
he lives at a secret location on the coast of
Europe, where his writing shack usually smells
of drying wetsuit (he's a former international
swimmer and an enthusiastic surfer).*